BART!

The Music and Lyrics of BART HOWARD

TRO HAMPSHIRE HOUSE PUBLISHING CORP.

COVER SKETCH BY JOE EULA

BART HOWARD, a native of Burlington, Iowa, reached New York in 1937 and, the following year, met Mabel Mercer the day she arrived in this country from her native England. At the suggestion of Marlene Dietrich, Miss Mercer sang one of the young composer's songs in her American debut at the Ruban Bleu. Later, after World War II, he served as her accompanist for four years before he went to the Blue Angel where he remained for eight years (1952-60) as pianist and *compere,* or host. Among the many singers who performed at the Blue Angel, a celebrated night club in those days, was Johnny Mathis, who became a particularly devoted champion of songs by Bart Howard. Peggy Lee was an early exponent of "In Other Words," and it was she who suggested changing the title officially to "Fly Me to the Moon," which was the way her listeners always identified the song. Meanwhile, of course, Mabel Mercer remained a faithful interpreter of his songs and a close personal friend until her death. Bart Howard's closest approach to Broadway came when he and Sam and Bell Spewack tried to make a musical based on the life of Gertrude Lawrence. The project did not work out, but two songs written for it, "Beware of the Woman" and "Who Besides You", are included in this collection. All in all, Bart Howard has written some 200 songs. Early in his career, he was taken to meet Cole Porter and played some of them for the older composer. Porter advised the young man to learn to sing them persuasively and, decades later Bart Howard did just that. At 73, accompanying himself at the piano, he made debuts singing his own songs in both concert and cabaret settings and found the experience to be heady indeed.

The Songs of BART HOWARD

Recorded by

Laurindo Almeida	Betty Johnson
Ames Bros.	Tom Jones
Buddy Barnes	Morgana King
Tony Bennett	Andre Kostelanetz
Ray Brown Trio	Barbara Lea
June Christy	Peggy Lee
Petula Clark	Norman Luboff
Nat King Cole	Mantovani
Cy Coleman	Johnny Mathis
Perry Como	Mabel Mercer
Chris Connor	Helen Merrill
Damita Jo	Wes Montgomery
Stuart Damon	Jane Morgan
Martha Davis	Portia Nelson
Charles De Forest	Peter Nero
Billy Eckstein	Anita O'Day
Eileen Farrell	Jimmy Roselli
Ferrante & Teicher	William Roy
Ella Fitzgerald	Felicia Sanders
Marvin Gaye	Bobby Short
Eydie Gorme	Frank Sinatra
Robert Goulet	K.T. Sullivan
Joe Harnell	Mel Torme
Ann Hathaway	Caterina Valente
Hampton Hawes	Sarah Vaughan
Hi Lo's	Dinah Washington
Lena Horne	Elizabeth Welch
	Julie Wilson

BEAUTIFUL WOMEN

Words and Music by
BART HOWARD

chorus:

IMAGINING THINGS

Words and Music by
BART HOWARD

Moderately with a beat

Im - ag-in-ing things, I love im - ag-in-ing things I could sit a - round by the hour star-ing

in - to space,_ Sniff-in' a flow'r with a smile on my face, Im - ag-in-ing things to do and plac-es to

see._____ Im - ag-in-ing things for you to do with me!_____

We toured the world in a pri-vate plane Stopped o - ver in sun-ny Spain_

To-ky-o "Vel-ly nice!"_ We stop there twice! While im - ag-in-ing things and whis-tling hill-bill-y

WHO BESIDES YOU

Words and Music by
BART HOWARD

Verse:

MY LOVE IS A WANDERER

Words and Music by
BART HOWARD

BEWARE OF THE WOMAN

Words and Music by
BART HOWARD

15

WHEN SOMEBODY CARES

Words and Music by
BART HOWARD

day_____ and it will nev-er get pneu-mon-ia, or so they say._____

When some-bod-y cares, for-tune o-pens ev-'ry door for you. When some-bod-y

cares, there's a whole new world in store for you! Some-bod-y holds your hand and

pres-to! You feel your whole life grow-ing rich-er know-ing:

WALK-UP

Words and Music by
BART HOWARD

BABY, GO AWAY NOW

Words and Music by
BART HOWARD

24

SELL ME!

Words and Music by
BART HOWARD

THANK YOU FOR THE LOVELY SUMMER

Words and Music by
BART HOWARD

YOUNG JUST ONCE

Words and Music by
BART HOWARD

Anatomy of A LOVE SONG

Words and Music by
BART HOWARD

WOULD YOU BELIEVE IT?

Words and Music by
BART HOWARD

Brightly

Verse:

I bought my-self a great big hat with a bright red feath-er and a bow.___ I

sold my stocks, bought some mink dyed fox, and I'm rid-in' high in-stead of hid-in' low.___ But re-

mem-ber the way I used to be, kind-a huff-y, plain stuff-y all the day.___ Never

IT WAS WORTH IT!
(That's What I'll Say)

Words and Music by
BART HOWARD

44

DON'T DREAM OF ANYBODY BUT ME

Words by
BART HOWARD

Music by
NEAL HEFTI

47

WELCOME HOME, ANGELINA

Words and Music by
BART HOWARD

I'VE GOT EVERYTHING

Words and Music by
BART HOWARD

Lyrics:
I've got ev-'ry-thing, ab-so-lute-ly ev-'ry-thing I'll ev-er need. I've got you! And you've got ev-'ry-thing, so I've got ev-'ry-thing I need!

PERFECT STRANGER

From Julius Monk's Downstairs Revue "TAKE FIVE"

Words and Music by
BART HOWARD

57

OVERTURE TO THE BLUES

Words and Music by
BART HOWARD

From the

mo-ment we met it was "boom"! Like there's mu-sic all o-ver the room.— vi-o-
sym-pho-ny up in the skies_ was for me and three oth-er guys._ So the
wom-an would come home to stay_ I could write up the score in a day._And if
lis-ten to some-thin' by Bach_ while I gaze at the hole in my sock._ Or just

lins_ sing-in' out_ with the news!_ I, well, I
stars_ in my eyes_ blew a fuse!_ They went
Bern-stein's still pay- in' his dues,_ there'd be
sit_ back and rock_ till I snooze!_ Guess I'm

WHERE DO YOU THINK YOU'RE GOING?

Words and Music by
BART HOWARD

Chorus

YEAR AFTER YEAR

Words and Music by
BART HOWARD

SO LONG AS HE LOVES YOU

Words and Music by
BART HOWARD

69

FLY ME TO THE MOON

(In Other Words)

Words and Music by
BART HOWARD